CW01475075

FOUNDATIONS OF SAMĀDHI

PART I OF PATAÑJALI'S YOGA SŪTRAS

समाधिपादः

samādhipādaḥ

I bow to the two lotus feet of the jungle physician, who eliminates the delusion caused by the poisonous herb of samsara. I prostrate before the Sage Patañjali in the form of a man holding a conch, wheel and sword.

© 2020 Saunak S. Nanavati

All rights reserved. No part of this publication may be reproduced, distributed, or transmitted in any form or by any means, including photocopying, recording, or other electronic or mechanical methods, without the prior written permission of the author, except in the case of brief quotations embodied in critical reviews and certain other noncommercial uses permitted by copyright law. For permission requests, write to the author, addressed "Attention: Permissions," at the address below.

Shaun Nanavati
198 S. Franklin Street
Nyack, N.Y. 10960

ISBN 9798684207792
Paperback

Authored by

पतञ्जलि - जाङ्गलिकायमाने

patañjali - jañgalikāyamāne

Patañjali, Jungle Physician

Translated by

Saunak S. Nanavati

Samuel S. Aldridge

PREFACE

At first glance, yet another translation of the *Yoga Sūtra* may seem unnecessary. Numerous translations already exist in libraries around the world. Respected Indian, British, and American scholars of religion and yoga practitioners have presented an intelligent and informed perspective. So, why offer another translation?

Rather than continue down the paths of previous traditions that utilize a religious or spiritual framework, this translation offers a practical perspective rooted in neuropsychology. Yoga is the *science* of attention. Attentional focus and emotional balance in the body are achieved through a better understanding of our mental processes. This translation makes the case that the true goal of yoga is to seek balance with one's environment.

Moreover, a neuropsychological interpretation of Patañjali's *Yoga Sūtra* moves closer to revealing the meaning he originally intended. If, as Quine notes in *Word and Object*,[1] we consider translation as "identity across linguistic systems," then this work is a kind of triple translation, seeking an identity

---

[1] W.O. Quine, *Word and Object* (Cambridge: MIT Press, 1960).

across spatial geography, a vast period of time, and "expressions of the body."[2]

It is important to note that Patañjali was a physician, not a priest. His perspective was informed by methods of observation, clinical examination, and empirical data. However, he also considered subjective experience to be a valid means of knowledge. In this way, one of the great contributions of Patañjali's *Yoga Sūtra* is that it provides a novel philosophical framework through which we can fully understand subtle biological phenomena, such as the nature of attention.

Patañjali's approach is also important in our current culture, where philosophies of the body are often dominated by two schools of thought that appear as opposites. One advocates a *hyper-materialism* that only considers measurable data as meaningful to the scientific study of consciousness. The other, *transcendental idealism*, privileges the subjective experience of an individual without examination. By introducing a method through which internal experience can be examined and validated, Patañjali creates a space where subjective experience is meaningfully integrated into the larger scientific project of consciousness studies. It is refreshing to discover a world-class mind with the humility to admit that consciousness is not limited to what is currently measured.

---

[2] Shigehisa Kuriyama, *The Expressiveness of the Body* (New York: Zone Books, 1999).

Patañjali's thinking about the human mind is therefore *not* a simple look to the past. It is a method and vision that orients us to the future of modern western psychological sciences. As our knowledge of the brain and consciousness continues to expand, advances in neuroscience provide a remarkable knowledge base for illuminating the teachings of these ancient traditions in their proper light. Instead of dismissing yogic philosophy as a mystic diversion or recreational practice at the periphery of western culture, it is now time for it to occupy the seat it has rightfully earned at the table of medical sciences.

As you read and reflect on the content in this book, let us honor the considerable scientific and clinical insights Patañjali provides. This is especially important in our current climate, where upheaval and disruption in our culture and politics call us to stop, reflect, and reconsider our inner and outer worlds. Patañjali's carefully considered framework provides a tool to maintain valid cognition that expands, rather than truncates, our individual and collective sense of health, wellbeing, and connection.

Saunak S. Nanavati

Nyack, N.Y. 2020

LINE 1

अथ योगानुशासनम् ।।१:१।।

atha yogānuśāsanam (1:1)
atha yoga-anu-śāsanam

atha: now
yoga: yoga
anu: following, after
śāsanam: systematic instruction

"Now (begins) the systematic instruction of yoga."

LINE 2

योगश्चित्तवृत्तिनिरोधः ।।१:२।।

yogascittavṛttinirodhaḥ (1:2)
yogaḥ-citta-vṛtti-nirodhaḥ

yogaḥ: yoga
citta: activity of mind
vṛtti: fluctuation
nirodhaḥ: inhibition, control

"Yoga is inhibition of the fluctuation of the mind's activity."

Like any good philosopher, Patañjali begins with a definition. He presents a framework of the mind in which an external stimulus causes mental activity to fluctuate. At its core, yoga is the ability to sustain focus of the mind despite distraction. This means you can practice yoga at any moment, and anything you do can become yoga. Patañjali's definition also provides a view of the brain's activity that parallels the one presented by Charles Sherrington[3] in the Western medical tradition. Specifically, the brain responds reflexively to stimuli in the environment while maintaining a steady, focused state through inhibition.

---

3 Sir Charles Sherrington, "Inhibition as a Coordinative Factor" (Nobel Lecture, Stockholm, December 10, 1932).

If the human body is inherently reflexive, then the key to a successful intervention for health and well-being starts with the inhibition of reflexive patterns. We cannot gain freedom of choice if we react without thought. In this way, the brain is mainly composed of inhibitory tracts. As our cortex becomes thicker, our ability to resist immediate responses improves. This inhibition also corresponds to specific electrical patterns in the brain.

Since this passage establishes the foundation for the entire text, its message requires attention. For the *Yoga Sūtra* to be considered a truly scientific text, we need empirically measurable definitions for specific states of mind. This will advance yoga immeasurably as a clinical science.

Dr. Richard Davidson's work with monks provides the basis for such a definition.[4] In one of the most famous scientific studies of meditation, Davidson measured the neural activity of meditators to discover a new type and pattern of electrical brain activity: synchronous gamma waves. He found that the electrical patterns in both hemispheres of the brain in long-term meditators moved

---

[4] Richard J. Davidson, Lawrence L. Greischar, Nancy B. Rawlings, Matthieu Ricard, and Antoine Lutz. "Long-Term Meditators Self-Induce High-Amplitude Gamma Synchrony during Mental Practice." *Proceedings of the National Academy of Sciences of the United States of America* 101, no. 46 (2004): 16369.

slowly and in synch. It is therefore suggested that if one is practicing yoga, then one's mental activity will also be moving in this direction.

While it is true that Patañjali did not have access to fMRI or EEG machines, he was nevertheless able to discern this cognitive state through close observation of his own mental processes combined with his knowledge of pulse diagnosis. Thus, his method is based in scientific measurement. He reached the same insights that we are only now *beginning* to attain with the technologies of modern measurement.

LINE 3

तदा द्रष्टुःस्वरूपेऽवस्थानम् ।।१:३।।

tadā draṣṭuḥsvarūpe'vasthānam (1:3)
tadā draṣṭuḥ sva-rūpe avasthānam

tadā: then
draṣṭuḥ: vision, understanding
sva-rūpe: one's true form
avasthānam: established

"Then understanding of one's true form is established."

When the mind is calm, the body does not respond to stimulus. It registers, observes, and considers. One who is in a yogic state pauses before action. The action may look exactly the same as one who acts reflexively, but the difference is that the true yogi acts from choice. Now, when behavior is no longer dictated by environmental stimuli, the mind remains calm and its true form is revealed.

It is important, however, to maintain caution. If the underlying perceptual apparatus is flawed, haunted by past mistakes or rife with bias, then self-analysis will be in error and the final course of action will be imprecise. A musician who has trained herself to play only what is written will have trouble improvising.

LINE 4

वृत्तिसारूप्यमितरत्र ।।१:४।।

vṛttisārūpyamitaratra (1:4)
vṛtti-sārūpyam-itaratra

vṛtti: mental conception, movements of mind
sārūpyam: true understanding, comprehension, same-formness
itaratra: misconception

"When the mind fluctuates, true understanding is replaced by misconception."

When the mind fluctuates, and the hemispheres produce conflicting signals, a misconception occurs. When the mind is calm, it can observe the environment carefully, pause and reflect before initiating synchronized action. This makes accurate observation the antidote to confusion.

The word "sārūpyam" literally means "same-formness," implying that the misleading distinctions of subject and object, me and you, are removed when the mind ceases to fluctuate. True understanding of reality arises in this stillness.

When observing one's own self within the context of natural processes, the notion of an individual unitary self in control of the outside world appears as an illusion. Our essential self is interdependent: it is defined in terms of our interactions with the environment, especially our relationships. As a child, we understand the world through the interpretive lens of our parents. For example, when a child falls, she immediately looks to her mother to orient herself to the experience. We interpret the world through others always, even if the other person is only represented internally. As we age, the voice of our parents continues to guide us. Our use of language also requires the internalization of the other. Thus, the dissolution between self and other is *not* a mystical experience. It is a simple observation of the natural world from another point of view.

When we see ourselves from a third-person standpoint, we can better adjust to the landscape of human interaction without the reactivity of the ego. When a child cries over spilled milk, a good mother will comfort her instead of becoming angry because the mother understands the larger context within which that emotion arises.

LINE 5

वृत्तयः पञ्चतय्यः क्लिष्टाक्लिष्टाः ।।१:५।।

vṛttayaḥ pañcatayyaḥ kliṣṭākliṣṭāḥ (1:5)
vṛttayaḥ-pañca-tayyaḥ-kliṣṭa-akliṣṭāḥ

vṛttayaḥ: directions of the mind
pañca: five
tayyaḥ: protection
kliṣṭa: harmful (involving afflictions, kleśas)
akliṣṭāḥ: beneficial (without afflictions)

"Yoga provides protection from the five directions of the mind, each of which can be beneficial or harmful."

Patañjali opens a new line of thinking here: scientifically defining the mind by its actions and qualities. This passage is key to understanding the next set of sutras, which further define the basis of the mind. At the same time, it is important to note the contextual nature of this sutra: no action is inherently good or bad. Each of the five directions can be beneficial or harmful.

LINE 6

प्रमाणविपर्ययविकल्पनिद्रास्मृतयः ॥१:६॥

pramāṇaviparyayavikalpanidrāsmṛtayaḥ (1:6)
pramāṇa-viparyaya-vikalpa-nidrā-smṛtayaḥ

pramāṇa: comprehension, insight, linear thought
viparyaya: recursive thinking
vikalpa: imagination
nidrā: sleep and dream
smṛtayaḥ: plural of smṛti, meaning "memory"

"The types of mental activity are insight, recursive thinking, imagination, sleep and dream, and memory."

This passage is straightforward. Patañjali now describes the mind's five directions. As he introduces each one in greater depth, we find that each of these directions can produce insight or error. According to this way of thinking, truth and error often arrive together, and true insight only arises when the signal is filtered from the noise.[5]

---

[5] To be clear, we realize that these definitions deviate from standard translations. If each of the movements of mind can be beneficial or harmful (1:5), how can knowledge be right or wrong? Thus, we move away from "right thought" toward "linear thinking." Similarly, we distance the definition of *viparayaya* from the moral category of miscomprehension to a purely descriptive, cognitive one of recursive thinking.

LINE 7

प्रत्यक्षानुमानागमाः प्रमाणानि ।।१:७।।

pratyakṣānumānāgamāḥ pramāṇāni (1:7)
pratyakṣa-anumāna-āgamāḥ pramāṇāni

pratyakṣa: direct experience through the senses
anumāna: cognition through inference
āgamāḥ: experience, authority of tradition
pramāṇāni: linear thought, comprehension, knowing (pl. of pramāṇa)

"The three ways of knowing are direct experience through the senses, cognition through inference, and the authority of previous experience."

This passage describes three ways of knowing phenomena in the world. First, through direct sensory experience. Second, through cognition based on inference. And finally, through the authority of tradition or instruction of one's teachers. Each of these methods can produce accurate knowledge, yet each of these approaches can also create errors. Authority is sometimes wrong. Inferences are subject to bias. And our senses can be fooled by illusion.

Ideally, the process of learning involves moving through each of these stages. When we are introduced to a subject, we often learn from the counsel of a wise teacher. However, as we engage more deeply, we understand complex processes by building a mental or physical model that combines information from various sources. In the final stage, we begin to develop our own hypotheses and engage directly with nature through our senses. Over time, we distill and use all of these methods to understand the nature of a phenomenon.

LINE 8

विपर्ययो मिथ्याज्ञानमतद्रूपप्रतिष्ठम् ।।१:८।।

viparyayo mithyājñānamatadrūpapratiṣṭham (1:8)
viparyaya mithyā-jñānam-atad-rūpa-pratiṣṭham

viparyaya: recursive thought
mithyā: contrarily, opposite
jñānam: perceptual knowledge, recognize
atad: not that
rūpa: form
pratiṣṭham: is based

"Recursive thinking is the opposite of perceptual knowledge established in the absence of form."

We practice recursive thinking every day as one of our core cognitive processes. To illustrate the benefits of this kind of thinking, a builder may create a house the second time with less effort by integrating information from their previous attempt. Or, a student can solve a math problem faster and with fewer steps the more they do it.

Perceptual knowledge is also often reflexive. When we bring perceptions into conscious awareness, we can adjust the repetitive, recursive processes of our mind so that our behavior comes under our control. In this way, we examine details, usually in our physical actions, to make them more efficient. Thus, as recursive thought becomes increasingly automatic, we are able to achieve our goals with greater ease.

Alternatively, if engaged incorrectly, recursive thinking may prove detrimental. This can be the case when someone takes longer to do something and the number of errors increase, as with an unhelpful obsession. In this instance, the same activity is repeated recursively without the ability to correctly assess how to improve the process. Like every mental activity, attention, action, and time must be understood *together* to determine the exact benefit or harm.

LINE 9

शब्दज्ञानानुपाती वस्तुशून्यो विकल्पः ।।१:९।।

śabdajñānānupātī vastuśūnyo vikalpaḥ (1:9)
śabda-jñāna-anupātī vastu-śunyaḥ vikalpaḥ

śabda: words/language
jñāna: knowledge
anupātī: following, sequence, close behind
vastu: foundation, object, item
śunyaḥ: empty, absent
vikalpa: imagination

"Imagination is knowledge of an object through words and expression in the absence of the object."

If we can conceive of an object that is not present, then we are using our imaginations. In Sanskrit, *vikalpa* is one of four types of imagination. It is the most basic category and requires no training. As we begin to meditate, we develop other types of imagination, which include *kalpana* (intentional mental creation), *pratibha* (spontaneous visionary insight), and *bhāvana* (yogic contemplation and envisioning). In each of these cases, no item or object is physically present though the mind is still focused on the sensory experience of one (i.e. image, sound, taste, etc.).

LINE 10

अभावप्रत्ययालम्बना वृत्तिर्निद्रा ।।१:१०।।

abhāvapratyayālambanā vṛttirnidrā (1:10)
abhāva-pratyaya-ālambanā vṛttiḥ-nidrā

abhāva: absence, non-existence
pratyaya: contents of mind, thought, bias, or object in focus
ālambanā: foundation, base, support
vṛttiḥ: movement of mind
nidrā: sleep and dream

"Sleep is the mental activity when no other content is present."

When we are sleeping, and not in a lucid dream, there is no other mental activity. Even when we remember a dream, it is just an act of memory rather than dreaming. Since we cannot readily observe when we are asleep, this mental state is defined by the absence of the other mental states (i.e. memory, imagination, recursive thought, and linear thought).

LINE 11

अनुभूतविषयासंप्रमोषः स्मृतिः ।।१:११।।

anubhūtaviṣayāsaṃpramoṣaḥ smṛtiḥ (1:11)
anubhūta-viṣaya-asaṃpramoṣaḥ smṛtiḥ

anubhūta: to come to or by, experienced, suffered
viṣaya: topic, issue, domain
asaṃpramoṣaḥ: the act of recollecting, holding, retaining
smṛtiḥ: memory

"Memory is the mental recollection of an issue previously experienced."

Memory is clearly defined as the mental production of previous experience. In a sense, every act of memory is also one of imagination, since we are comprehending an object or an experience that is not present. However, memory is different from imagination because memory is grounded in previous sense impressions and those episodes that collectively compose reality. Imagination is *not* bound by previous events.

Memory can be beneficial or harmful. While it can prevent us from making the same mistakes, a painful memory can also cause us to avoid an opportunity or repeat a compulsion. Alternatively, though no less significant, a pleasurable memory can lead to an endless cycle of grasping and disappointment.

LINE 12

अभ्यासवैराग्याभ्यां तन्निरोधः ।।१:१२।।

abhyāsavairāgyābhyāṃ tannirodhaḥ (1:12)
abhyāsa-vairāgya-abhyāṃ tad-nirodhaḥ

abhyāsa: practice, striving, repetition
vairāgya: letting go, proper discrimination
abhyāṃ: indicates a dual ending
tad: that (the yogic state)
nirodhaḥ: inhibition, cessation

"Yoga is the cessation of the process of striving and letting go."

Patañjali has completed his initial definitions and now directs our attention toward the processes of yoga. The initial stage involves pausing our reflexive response to objects in the environment. We strive and we let go in an endless cycle of approach-and-withdrawal. We are easily moved in one direction or another by desire, sensory experience, and the influence of others, which impact our mental activity. If we can maintain control over our responses, then the influence of grasping and aversion will fade. Decisions will stop being reflexive and freedom can be attained through conscious choice.

LINE 13

तत्र स्थितौ यत्नोऽभ्यासः ।।१:१३।।

tatra sthitau yatno'bhyāsaḥ (1:13)
tatra sthitau yatnaḥ-abhyāsaḥ

tatra: in that case, then
sthitau: being established, firm (locative case)
yatnaḥ: effort
abhyāsa: practice

"Meditative absorption emerges with steady effort and practice."

In this context, *abhyāsa* refers to the practice or repetition of yogic meditation so that we can enter into a state of deep absorption. Regular and steady effort is required. This is non-negotiable. For a change to occur, so that *any* type of behavior becomes automatic, it must be repeated with steady effort. In this way, repetition creates "neuroplasticity," which is the brain's ability to develop new connections. These connections are driven by repeated and focused sensory engagement with the environment.

Moreover, meditation grows inhibitory tracks throughout different regions of the cortex, so that even when an action appears to be activated, it is the *disinhibition* of the reflex that is occurring. For example, if you stroke a baby's palm with your finger, the baby will reflexively grasp your finger (the Babinski Reflex).[6] As a child's frontal lobe develops, however, the child can choose not to grasp when their hand is stroked. Thus, an open palm that appears still, is actually the result of an intentional choice to inhibit. So also with speech, silence can be an act of inhibition. When applied in the appropriate context, silence displays eloquence.

6 *Merriam-Webster.com Dictionary*, s.v. "Babinski reflex," accessed September 2, 2020, https://www.merriam-webster.com/dictionary/Babinski%20reflex.

LINE 14

स तु दीर्घकालनैरन्तर्यसत्कारासेवितो दृढभूमिः

||१:१४||

sa tu dīrghakālanairantaryasatkārāsevito dṛḍhabhūmiḥ (1:14)
sa tu dīrgha-kāla-nairantarya-sat-kāra-āsevitaḥ dṛḍha-bhūmiḥ

sa: along, with
tu: you
dīrgha: slow, deep, long
kāla: time
nairantarya: constant, uninterrupted
sat: true essence
kāra: maker, doer
āsevitaḥ: performed, repeated
dṛḍha: strong, tight, firm(ly)
bhūmiḥ: earth, soil, effort, grounded

"This meditative absorption becomes naturally established with strong, grounded, and consistent effort over time."

While this passage reads like a simple, commonsense maxim, it also highlights an important principle of neuroplasticity. Namely, a single behavior free from all distractions, combined with steady effort, actually *changes* the structure of the brain, so one's will is less necessary after a period of time. Though effort is a primary condition, effort alone is not enough. Refined attention must therefore be coordinated with a motor action that is synchronized with controlled sensory input. The next two lines of the *sutra* explain this principle in greater depth.

LINE 15

दृष्टानुश्रविकविषयवितृष्णस्य वशीकारसंज्ञावैराग्यम्

॥१:१५॥

dṛṣṭānuśravikaviṣayavitṛṣṇasya vaśīkārasaṃjñāvairāgyaṃ (1:15)
dṛṣṭa-anuśravika-viṣaya-vitṛṣṇasya vaśī-kāra-saṃjñā-vairāgyaṃ

dṛṣṭa: vision, observation, experienced
anuśravika: that which is heard, "spoken tradition," scripture
viṣaya: subject, category, issue, theme
vitṛṣṇasya: absence of thirst or craving
vaśī: sound
kāra: maker, doer, author
saṃjñā: designation, agreement, harmony
vairāgyaṃ: state of proper discrimination

"In the state of proper discrimination, all cravings are absent and harmony is achieved between the inner voice and that which is heard and envisioned."

In *The Apology*[7] by Plato, when Socrates is on trial for subverting the youth of Athens, the prosecuting attorney asks if his *daemon*, or inner voice, tells him what to do. To

[7] Bertand Russell, *Wisdom of the West* (Garden City, NY: Doubleday, 1959), p.83.

this he replies: "No, it only tells me what *not* to do." His inner voice is essentially inhibitory. Socrates then fires a parting shot: "That's why I never entered politics."

This *vaśīkāra,* or "inner voice," is the "author of sound," which allows for internal dialogue and reconciliation of differing positions. When one separates signal from noise, one experiences the fluid integration of one's inner voice with the outer environment.

LINE 16

तत्परं पुरुषख्यातेर्गुणवैतृष्ण्यम् ।।१:१६।।

tatparaṃ puruṣakhyāterguṇavaitṛṣṇyaṃ (1:16)

tat-paraṃ puruṣa-khyāteḥ-guṇa-vaitṛṣṇyaṃ

tat: that

paraṃ: absolute, ultimate, highest

puruṣa: parasympathetic-mediated, inner voice or self

khyāteḥ: understanding

guṇa[8]: dynamic forces of the environment

vaitṛṣṇyaṃ: state of non-craving

---

[8] *Guna* is defined in Vedanta philosophy as one of the three main qualities of nature: *tamas* (passive), rajas (active), and *sattvic* (balanced). These qualities can be internal or external. If we were to assign individual nervous system qualities to the *gunas* (dynamic forces), these would be balanced (*sattva*), sympathetically-dominant (*rajas*), and parasympathetically-dominant (*tamas*). This is a process-oriented system, in which the goal of health is a balanced state.

How does one become aware of one's internal state? Pulse diagnosis provides a useful guide. Patañjali used this technique to measure the fluctuations in one's internal life.. As a physician, Patañjali further discerned unique patterns, integrating both subjective experience and observations of others. Thus, *purusa* (subjective experience mediated by the parasympathetic nervous system) and *prakriti* (the subjective analogue of the sympathetic nervous system) contain an element that is physiological in nature.

In this view, the parasympathetic nervous system regulates attention and coordinates inhibition of somatic reflexes. *Puruṣa* is inner speech with a physiological component. *Purusa* comes from within and controls how we respond to our environment. *Prakriti* determines the individual alertness and intensity of our response.

"One who has achieved the highest awareness of the inner self craves nothing and is not influenced by the dynamic forces of the environment."

Once we are able to control and ground our mental states in a balanced manner, the external changes that affect the body will not impact the mind. We become a flame that the wind cannot extinguish. However, this is not achieved by being immutable. To the contrary, our stability emerges from the ability to make adjustments in real-time as the environment shifts. These adjustments, in turn, allow us to maintain a steady, balanced state.

Here we are presented with the signs of one who has awakened and achieved a mental state free of fluctuations. Once craving is abolished, nothing in the environment can impact the steady mind. It is important to note, however, that we still bear the influence of past experience. Transcending physical and mental craving therefore does not imply total resolution of these forces. Rather, it is one step along the path toward enlightenment.

LINE 17

वितर्कविचारानन्दास्मितानुगमात् संप्रज्ञातः ।।१:१७।।

vitarkavicārānandāsmitānugamāt saṃprajñātaḥ (1:17)
vitarka-vicāra-ānanda-asmitā-anugamāt saṃprajñātaḥ

vitarka: logic
vicāra: reflection, discrimination
ānanda: bliss
asmitā: total absorption
anugamāt: following from
saṃprajñātaḥ: high state of samadhi or attentional focus

"The highest state of attentional focus emerges over stages: first logically, second through reflection and discrimination, third in bliss and tranquility, and finally through total absorption."

By mastering attention, we come to understand how we learn. Let us take the example of translating a foreign text into our native language. First, we seek to understand the rules of grammar and vocabulary. Then we apply this information to the text itself, which requires significant cognitive effort. After using the logic of grammar and vocabulary to complete the task of translation, we reflect on certain passages and gain a more nuanced understanding of the author's meaning. We gain insight into where and when certain rules are not applicable.

As language becomes spontaneous, the cognitive demands greatly lessen and the expression of a new language takes on a blissful quality. Emotion is engaged and we begin to master a new skill. In advanced stages, language becomes automatic as the cognitive understanding of grammar becomes completely internalized. Effort is no longer required as we achieve a state of linguistic flow.

Saṃprajñātaḥ is the highest achievement of yoga, a state in which one is observing what is happening in the environment and applying a specific attentional process to that situation. In certain moments, cognitive examination may be required again to understand a new phrase. Or one may need to reflect and discriminate between two words where a previous misunderstanding existed. The highest goal is not the state of total and spontaneous absorption. Rather, it is the ability to identify the right attentional tool to meet the immediate needs of the environment.

LINE 18

विरामप्रत्ययाभ्यासपूर्वः संस्कारशेषोऽन्यः ।।१:१८।।

virāmapratyayābhyāsapūrvaḥ saṃskāraśeṣo'nyaḥ (1:18)
virāma-pratyaya-abhyāsa-pūrvaḥ saṃskāra-śeṣaḥ'anyaḥ

virāma: complete cessation, synchronized EEG gamma frequency
pratyaya: "wandering of mind," random movement of mental activity
abhyāsa: practice, repetition, contextually-driven
pūrvaḥ: earlier, the past
saṃskāra: unmanifested impression
śeṣaḥ: memories of past, residue
anyaḥ: the other

"While present mental impulses will cease with practice, memories of the past and their effects linger."

Once the mind stabilizes within its environment and is no longer subject to external impulses, internal obstacles remain. Memories are the last remnant of our reflexive cognitive patterns and often the most difficult to overcome. To understand whether a specific memory is beneficial or harmful, one must be able to examine one's own internal cognition and determine whether and when it is valid. This is the framework for a new stage of self-analysis, which will now be introduced.

LINE 19

भवप्रत्ययो विदेहप्रकृतिलयानाम् ।।१:१९।।

bhavapratyayo videhaprakṛtilayānām (1:19)
bhava-pratyaya videha-prakṛti-layānām

bhava: origin, genesis, prosperity
pratyaya: true perception, insight, ascertainment
videha: beyond the body and the senses
prakṛti: nature, natural constitution
layānām: awareness of, absorbed in

"True insight beyond the body and senses emerges through absorption in one's natural constitution."

This line is a natural extension of Sutra 1:17. The final state of *samādhi* can be most easily attained through the philosophic realization that insight arrives by moving beyond identification with the physical body. Our biases naturally fall away in this state of being, leaving us with true insight into our intrinsic nature. The alternative is evident when comparing the same experience of two people with different biases. One who is depressed may see a glass as half empty, while one who is optimistic may see the glass as half full. Clear insight sees it as half.

LINE 20

श्रद्धावीर्यस्मृतिसमाधिप्रज्ञापूर्वक इतरेषाम् ॥१:२०॥

śraddhāvīryasmṛtisamādhiprajñāpūrvaka itareṣām (1:20)
śraddhā-vīrya-samādhi-prajñā-pūrvaka itareṣām

śraddhā: faith and trust
vīrya: enthusiasm, vigor, heroism
smṛti: clear recollection
samādhi-prajñā: awareness, intuition, penetrating wisdom
pūrvaka: to precede
itareṣām: of others

"Trust, enthusiasm, and memory all precede penetrating wisdom."

Regular practice, despite distractions, requires trust in the process. This is not a blind faith, but an understanding that the process of yoga works in a certain way, consistently and reliably. Next, enthusiastic effort is added. Emotion can provide an invaluable boost. Lastly, one needs to keep lessons learned in one's mind and utilize memory so that one's effort is not squandered. As one practices and develops one's attention, a deep, penetrating wisdom emerges. This established wisdom is evident in one's behaviors, actions, and thoughts. This wisdom eventually becomes automatic.

LINE 21

तीव्रसंवेगानामासन्नः ॥१:२१॥

tīvrasaṃvegānāmāsannaḥ (1:21)
tīvra-saṃvegānām-āsannaḥ

tīvra: acute
saṃvegānam: speed, intensity
āsannaḥ: very near

"The more intense the effort, the closer the goal."

There is no magic bullet or blue pill for the achievement of mental discipline. All the knowledge in the world is still limited by the intensity of the effort employed. The more intense the effort toward one's goal, the closer the goal becomes. This effort is not a blind spasm of energy. Rather, the effort is focused within the roadmap Patañjali provides.

LINE 22

मृदुमध्याधिमात्रत्वात्ततोऽपि विशेषः ।।१:२२।।

mṛdumadhyādhimātratvāttato'pi viśeṣaḥ (1:22)
mṛdu-madhya-adhimātra-vāt-tataḥ-api viśeṣaḥ

mṛdu: mild
madhya: medium
adhimātra: intense
vāt: or
tataḥ: this
api: also
viśeṣaḥ: level, differentiation

"The results of this practice also vary according to the level of effort: mild, medium, or intense."

Results will vary depending on your effort. Each path has its own integrity, yet effort is a key underlying factor in the fruit that will be produced. The degree of one's intensity is a combination of individual *prakṛti* and *puruṣa.* Thus, one's control of one's level of energy in terms of both tempo and intensity is a foundational factor in the attainment of attentional control.

LINE 23

ईश्वरप्रणिधानाद्वा ।।१:२३।।

īśvarapraṇidhānādvā (1:23)
īśvara-praṇidhānāt-vā

īśvara: the environment, nature
praṇidhānāt: submission, balance, "laying it all down"
vā: alternatively

"The state of yoga is achieved through balance with the environment."

The natural environment that surrounds us is the ultimate teacher. One can either accept this basic reality or attempt to assert one's will, in vain, against it. The ego imposes one's will on the environment at the cost of great energy. An alternative path is to observe with objectivity, carefully assess the situation, and then take action with clear intention. The goal is to achieve balance with the environment rather than attempt to control it through force of will.

Īśvara is often translated as a monotheistic "God." By understanding *īśvara* as the "natural environment," the notion of authority can be relinquished and a broader goal of synchrony with the environment takes the place of obedience.

LINE 24

क्लेशकर्मविपाकाशयैरपरामृष्टः पुरुषविशेष ईश्वरः

।।१:२४।।

kleśakarmavipākāśayairaparāmṛṣṭaḥ puruṣaviśeṣa īśvaraḥ (1:24)
kleśa-karma-vipāka-āśayaiḥ-aparāmṛṣṭaḥ puruṣa-viśeṣa īśvaraḥ

kleśa: obstacle, covering
karma: action, deed
vipāka: impact of action, consequences
āśayaiḥ: residue of past action
aparāmṛṣṭaḥ: unaffected
puruṣa: attention, parasympathetic nervous system
viśeṣa: level, differentiation, special attribute
īśvaraḥ: environment

"(In a state of yoga) the degree of synchrony between the attention and the environment is unaffected by obstacles, actions, impacts, and residues of past events."

When one is truly present, one can let go of the cumulative brushstrokes on one's personality. Mizuta Masahide illustrates this point in this haiku:

"Since my house burned down
I now have a better view
of the rising moon."[9]

Pure embodied presence sheds memory and its biases. This relationship between attention and environment overrides all other concerns. Obstacles, actions, consequences, and residues of past events evaporate, leaving you with an unobstructed view of your own nature.

---

9 "Quotable Quote," Quote by Mizuta Masahide, Goodreads, accessed September 2, 2020. https://www.goodreads.com/quotes/631601-since-my-house-burned-down-i-now-have-a-better

LINE 25

तत्र निरतिशयं सर्वज्ञबीजम् ।।१:२५।।

tatra niratiśayaṃ sarvajñabījam (1:25)
tatra niratiśayaṃ sarvajña-bījam

tatra: that
niratiśayaṃ: highest, unmatched
sarvajña: all knowing, omniscient
bījam: seed

"The seed of all knowledge is contained within the sublime environment."

Everything is contained in nature, of which we are all part. *Īśvara* is not supernatural because nothing is outside our natural world. The environment begins and ends all things. Only the delusion of our own omnipotence prevents this self-evident observation. The natural world provides the basis of all knowledge.

LINE 26

स एष पूर्वेषामपि गुरुः कालेनानवच्छेदात् ।।१:२६।।

sa eṣa pūrveṣāmapi guruḥ kālenānavacchedāt (1:26)
sa eṣa pūrveṣāṃ-api guruḥ kālena-anavacchedāt

sa: it (the environment)
eṣa: eternal
pūrveṣāṃ: of the ancients
api: also
guruḥ: teacher
kāla (ena): (by) time
anavacchedāt: due to indivisibility, unconditioned

"The environment, unconditioned by time, is the teacher of all teachers, even the ancients."

Leonardo da Vinci says: "He who has access to the fountain does not go to the water-pot."[10] One does not need to go to a teacher if one can observe the environment directly, for this is the original fountain from which every great teacher drinks. The true source of all wisdom is a keen observation of the environment.

---

10 Leonardo da Vinci, *Leonardo Da Vinci on Painting: A Lost Book* (California: University of California Press, 1965), 32.

LINE 27

तस्य वाचकः प्रणवः ।।१:२७।।

tasya vācakaḥ praṇavaḥ (1:27)

tasya: its
vācakaḥ: verbal symbol, expression, words
praṇavaḥ: symbol OṂ ॐ

"Its expression is the symbol OṂ."

If we think of OṂ as the basic unit of vibration from which all sound derives, much as individual colors are derived from white light, then this passage takes on far greater significance. OṂ is the expression of the environment's state of being from the microscopic to the cosmic. This is evident from the constant vibration of cells, to the harmonic resonance of wind in the forest, to the residual hum of the Big Bang. Once we begin to listen carefully, we soon realize that the environment is vibrational at its source and thus energetically creative.

LINE 28

तज्जपस्तदर्थभावनम् ।।१:२८।।

tajjapastadarthabhāvanam (1:28)
tad-japaḥ-tad-artha-bhāvanam

tad: that (OṂ)
japaḥ: vocal repetition
tad: that (OṂ)
artha: meaning
bhāvanam: direct knowledge, cognition, perception, experience

"Direct experience of its meaning is assisted by vocal repetition."

By training the brain to recognize a particular frequency with intense and prolonged repetition, a symbol becomes intelligible because the corresponding sound to the symbol is at last perceived. A clear illustration of this principle is found in a classic study of neuroplasticity. Michael Merzenich[11] realized that the brains of children with phonological dyslexia were unable to recognize particular

[11] Michael Merzenich et al, "Neural deficits in children with dyslexia ameliorated by behavioral remediation: Evidence from functional MRI." *Proceedings of the National Academy of Sciences* 100, no. 5 (2003): 2860-2865.

sounds and match them with their corresponding symbols due to an ear infection during the crucial developmental stage (ages 18-36 months). By coordinating a sound with a visual symbol, he cured the phonological dyslexia in school-age children.

An analogue to the dyslexic child is present for each of us, for whom natural harmonics are a strange language. Vocal repetition of OṂ, a harmonic sound from which other waveforms are derived, provides a way to prime ourselves so we can understand the symbols of nature's processes. By using our voices, we can attune ourselves to the vibration of the natural environment. Our bodies become instruments.

LINE 29

ततः प्रत्यक्चेतनाधिगमोऽप्यन्तरायाभावश्च ।।१:२९।।

tataḥ pratyakcetanādhigamo'pyantarāyābhāvaśca (1:29)
tataḥ pratyak-cetanā-adhigamaḥ-api-antar-āya-abhāvaḥ-ca

tataḥ: from that
pratyak: in the opposite direction, inwardly
cetanā: mind, self-awareness, spirit, will
adhigamaḥ: attainment, approach, obtainment
api: also
antarāya: distraction, obstacle
abhāvaḥ: absence, non-existence, destruction
ca: and

"That practice results in the mind turning inward and the destruction of distractions."

This first section of the *Yoga Sutra* describes the steps necessary for developing *samādhi*, a state of refined awareness. The passage above begins a brief section on overcoming distractions and obstacles along the way. Patañjali discusses the types of distraction, along with their assessment and annihilation, in the following sutras.

Our goal is to repeat this process of attuning ourselves to the environment. In so doing, we train our minds to become so stable that distractions lose their ability to hijack our attentional focus.

LINE 30

व्याधिस्त्यानसंशयप्रमादालस्याविरतिभ्रान्तिदर्शनालब्ध-
भूमिकत्वानवस्थितत्वानि चित्तविक्षेपास्तेऽन्तरायाः

।।१:३०।।

vyādhistyānasaṃśayapramādālasyāviratibhrāntidarśanālabd
bhūmikatvānavasthitatvāni cittavikṣepāste'ntarāyāḥ (1:30)

vyādhi-styāna-saṃśaya-pramāda-ālasya-avirati-bhrānti-darśana-
alabdha-bhūmikatva-anavasthitatvāni citta-vikṣepaḥ-te-
antarāyāḥ

vyādhi: physical illness
styāna: confusion, indolence
saṃśaya: doubt
pramāda: carelessness
ālasya: lethargy, fatigue
avirati: overindulgence
bhrānti-darśana: delusion, erroneous perception
alabdha-bhūmikatva: lack of effort
anavasthitatvāni: inability to stay still
citta: mind, consciousness
vikṣepaḥ: confusion, distraction
te: those
antarāyāḥ: distractions, impediments

"Those distractions and obstacles of the mind are: 1) physical and mental disease, 2) ethical confusion, 3) self-doubt, 4) carelessness in action, 5) fatigue, 6) overindulgence in material pleasure, 7) erroneous perception, 8) lack of effort, and 9) inability to stay still."

In the thirtieth sutra, Patañjali begins a new line of thinking: self-analysis. He begins by articulating the schema of distractions, or obstacles, to stabilizing and refining attention. While most of us are familiar with all nine, we may not initially recognize them as distractions. Whether consciously or otherwise, many often strive toward them! Therefore, by first identifying the distractions, we can begin the work of understanding how each may impede our progress and remove them appropriately. If we are ready, we can respond to these distractions as the matador redirects the bull.

LINE 31

दुःखदौर्मनस्याङ्गमेजयत्वश्वासप्रश्वासा विक्षेपसहभुवः

॥१:३१॥

duḥkhadaurmanasyāṅgamejayatvaśvāsapraśvāsā vikṣepasahabhuvaḥ (1:31)

duḥkha-daurmanasya-aṅgam-ejayatva-śvāsa-praśvāsāḥ vikṣepa-saha-bhuvaḥ

duḥkha: distress, anxiety, pain
daurmanasya: lack of mental peace
aṅgam: body
ejayatva: shaking, tremors of the body
śvāsa: breathing
praśvāsāḥ: disordered breathing
vikṣepa: distracted
saha: with
bhuvaḥ: manifestations

"Pain, lack of mental peace, shaking of the body, and disordered breathing are manifestations of a distracted mind."

Patañjali again lays out the physical symptoms of a distracted mind. He provides diagnostic criteria for clearly identifying when the mind is bound by obstacles. Once the mental contributions of a disordered state are known, the distracted mind can be isolated and treated as the cause of the issue. This is in contrast to a materialist philosophy of medicine in which the body is understood as the cause of pain, disordered breathing, tremors, and a lack of mental peace.

LINE 32

तत्प्रतिषेधार्थमेकतत्त्वाभ्यासः ।।१:३२।।

tatpratiṣedhārthamekatattvābhyāsaḥ (1:32)
tad-pratiṣedha-artham-eka-tattva-abhyāsaḥ

tad: it
pratiṣedha: prohibits
artham: for the purpose of
eka: one
tattva: reality, principle, nature
abhyāsaḥ: practice, repetition

"Distractions of the mind are negated with steady practice on the essential nature of an object."

This sutra opens a new set of ideas: the intervention, or antidote, to the distracted mind. The previous two sutras provide the means for the correct assessment of one's mental state. In the following passages, Patañjali will systematically lay out the necessary social, physiological, and attentional steps for achieving a focused mental state.

If the steady mind is the antidote to our distracted mental state, how can we go about achieving stability?

Through the practice of pausing and allowing the reflexive impulse to pass. If one pauses, then one can see a phenomenon through various lenses. Through this process, the underlying causes of symptoms are revealed. We can quickly determine and delineate those objects in our environment that are beneficial to our ongoing growth and those which are not. It is then our responsibility to choose our response wisely and with care.

As this process is repeated, the manner in which the mind internalizes an object in the environment reveals one of the unique qualities of the mind. Thus begins *meta-cognition*, the process of becoming aware of, and thinking about, the manner in which one thinks.

LINE 33

मैत्रीकरुणामुदितोपेक्षाणां सुखदुःखपुण्यापुण्यविषयाणां
भावनातश्चित्तप्रसादनम् ।।१:३३।।

maitrīkaruṇāmuditopekṣāṇāṃ (1:33)
sukhaduḥkhapuṇyāpuṇyaviṣayāṇāṃ bhāvanātaścittaprasādanam

maitrī: friendliness
karuṇā: compassion
mudit: joy
upekṣā: indifference
āṇāṃ: (plural case)
sukha: happiness
duḥkha: suffering
puṇya: virtuous
apuṇya: error-prone
viṣaya: subject
bhāvana: yogic contemplation
taḥ: they, all of them
citta-prasādanam: calm mind

"Maintain friendliness toward the happy, compassion toward the suffering, joy toward the virtuous, and indifference toward the error-prone, in order to maintain a calm mind."

These four precepts of social functioning offer a simple roadmap for preventing relationships from becoming distractions. They provide a way to pursue healthy interactions regardless of the behavior of others.

Social relationships can be complicated. It is a natural tendency to diagnose or blame others when we experience disruptive behavior. This can create distress in a relationship. If confronted and engaged, however, this distress can be transformed into an opportunity for connection and understanding. By adjusting our behavior in response to the issue at hand, we can create harmony with the other.

It is important to understand the other person, their needs, and the type of action that will benefit both parties. For example, practicing compassion toward the error-prone can lead to an unfruitful investment of time and resources. We can therefore apply these four approaches to every social situation and note how they lead to greater harmony in relationships with friends, family, foes, and strangers.

LINE 34

प्रच्छर्दनविधारणाभ्यां वा प्राणस्य ।।१:३४।।

pracchardanavidhāraṇābhyāṃ vā prāṇasya (1:34)
pracchardana-vidhāraṇābhyāṃ vā prāṇasya

pracchardana: forceful exhalation
vidhāraṇābhyāṃ: conscious control, practice, repetition
vā: or
prāṇasya: breathing consciously

"The mind is stabilized by forceful exhalation or conscious retention of the breath."

In the previous sutra, Patañjali articulated the social conditions for stabilizing the mind. Now he highlights the most important physiological factor: specific breathing patterns. Breathing exercises are powerful tools for developing the capacity to amplify or inhibit mental activity.

Patañjali previously described the four parts of the breath: inhale, exhale, and the pauses in between. The pauses can be long or short. Inhalations and exhalations can be forceful or weak as well as deep or shallow. Breathing and thinking are deeply intertwined; the management of one leads to the control of the other. Equipped with these building blocks of breath, one can construct specific combinations to gain specific mental results.

LINE 35

विषयवती वा प्रवृत्तिरुत्पन्ना मनसस्थितिनिबन्धनी

।।१:३५।।

viṣayavatī vā pravṛttirutpannā manasasthitinibandhanī (1:35)
viṣayavatī vā pravṛttiḥ-utpannā manasaḥ-sthiti-nibandhanī

viṣayavatī: full of sense perception
vā: or
pravṛttiḥ: inclination, propensity, tendency
utpannā: arisen, born
manasaḥ: mental
sthiti: stage, state
nibandhanī: binding, fastening

"Or (the stabilization of attention) arises from awareness of the propensity of the mind to bind to sense experience."

The greatest obstacle to steady attention is found in the pleasure and/or pain of sense experience. We grasp for what is pleasurable and avoid what is painful. There is a propensity of the mind to fool itself when we identify with our emotional experience. Hence, if one understands how the mind can be deceived by its own mechanisms, one gains greater insight into the repercussions of previous actions.

In this way, we can quickly learn when to approach and when to withdraw from specific people, places, and things. In order to achieve this level of discernment, however, it is crucial to avoid projecting our fears, expectations, or wishes from the past onto the present. By becoming aware of the potential for misperception, we can learn to act with greater clarity and ease.

LINE 36

विशोका वा ज्योतिष्मती ।।१:३६।।

viśokā vā jyotiṣmatī (1:36)
viśokā vā jyotiṣmatī

viśokā: free from grief, unhappiness
vā: or
jyotiṣmatī: pervaded by a state of clear light

"Or a state of mind pervaded by clear light can free an individual from grief and unhappiness."

One of the definitions of *jyotiṣmatī* is "luminous, bright or shining."[12] On such a night one can easily see the path. Similarly, when one is in a clear state of mind, the path of action is illuminated and your decisions are healthy. We all experience this at different points in our lives. Knowing how to be in this state *at will* is the goal of yoga practice.[13]

---

[12] Vanam Shvaram Apte, *The Practical Sanskrit-English Dictionary* (Kyoto: Rinsen Press, 1957), p. 357.

[13] It is also interesting to note that *jyotiṣmatī* is the name of a particular medicinal herb in Ayurvedic medicine that is believed to enlighten the mind. Similarly, this mental practice relieves one from the suffering caused by the poisons of a distracted mind.

LINE 37

वीतरागविषयं वा चित्तम् ।।१:३७।।

vītarāgaviṣayaṃ vā cittam (1:37)
vīta-rāga-viṣayaṃ vā cittam

vīta: approach eagerly, attainment
rāga: color, affection, passion, melody
viṣayaṃ: place
vā: or
cittam: consciousness

"Or by contemplating the mind of a transcendent teacher."

This passage provides more solid advice for stabilizing the mind: seek the counsel of a teacher who has achieved the goal you seek. Or, like those who practice Guru Yoga, visualize the beatific mind of your teacher in order to harmonize your own thoughts. A transcendent teacher possesses more than technical knowledge. He or she provides the emotional experience of being in a loving home, a place of affection, which we eagerly seek and approach. It is the intrigue of embodied wisdom that draws us to the transcendent teacher.

LINE 38

स्वप्ननिद्राज्ञानालम्बनं वा ।।१:३८।।

svapnanidrājñānālambanaṃ vā (1:38)
svapna-nidrā-jñāna-ālambanaṃ vā

svapna: dream, sleep
nidrā: deeply relaxed state
jñāna: deep knowledge, inquiry, wisdom, pattern-awareness
ālambanaṃ: support
vā: or

"Or support for the stabilized mind can come from inquiry and deep knowledge into sleep, dream, and a deeply relaxed mental state."

Freud states that "dreams are the royal road to the unconscious."[14] Patañjali is saying something similar here, but expanding beyond dream analysis into mental visualization that occurs during states of deep relaxation. If one seeks awareness of the nature of the mind, one can also explore the images through which emotion and perception interact.

[14] Sigmund Freud, *Interpretation of Dreams,* trans. Dr. A. A. Brill (New York: Modern Library Edition, 1994), 459.

LINE 39

यथाभिमतध्यानाद्वा ।।१:३९।।

yathābhimatadhyānādvā (1:39)
yathā-abhimata-dhyānāt-vā

yathā: as, because, since
abhimata: wish, desire, curiosity
dhyānāt: contemplation, for meditating
vā: or

"Or contemplation on any object of curiosity can calm the mind."

Any topic in and of itself is not as important as one's wish to understand and explore the topic. The creative desire to engage in inquiry calms the mind. *Abhimata* adds a sense of emotional engagement to the act of contemplation, thereby fusing one's emotional and cognitive states of being.

LINE 40

परमाणुपरममहत्त्वान्तोऽस्य वशीकारः ।।१:४०।।

paramāṇuparamamahattvānto'sya vaśīkāraḥ (1:40)
paramāṇu-parama-mahattva-antaḥ-asya vaśīkāraḥ

paramāṇu: primal atom, smallest
parama: ultimate
mahattva: importance
antaḥ: end, extension
asya: his, her
vaśīkāraḥ: inner voice, "author of sound"

"In this state of deep absorption, in tune with your inner voice, everything from the smallest atom of the microcosm to the greatest expanse of the macrocosm is within the bounds of comprehension."

Patañjali is speaking to a unique type of knowledge: *gnosis,* which can be translated as *intuition.* When intuition is developed, insight into the nature of the world is within one's grasp. This is based upon the view that one's conscious and unconscious processes are aspects of the larger world. Thus, when one is carefully attuned to one's inner voice, greater knowledge and insight emerge.

LINE 41

क्षीणवृत्तेरभिजातस्येव मणेर्ग्रहीतृग्रहणग्राह्येषु
तत्स्थतदञ्जनता समापत्तिः ।।१:४१।।

kṣīṇavṛtterabhijātasyeva maṇergrahītṛgrahaṇagrāhyeṣu
tatsthatadañjanatā samāpattiḥ (1:41)
kṣīṇa-vṛtteḥ-abhijātasya-iva maṇeḥ-grahītṛ-grahaṇa-grāhyeṣu
tatstha-tadañjanatā samāpattiḥ

kṣīṇa: weakened, dwindled
vṛtteḥ: fluctuations of the mind
abhijātasya: of royal birth, flawless
iva: like
maṇeḥ: of a crystal
grahītṛ: perceiver, knower
grahaṇa: knowledge
grāhyeṣu: in knowledge
tatstha: that which is not revealed
tadañjanatā: that background
samāpattiḥ: refined attention

"When the mind is still, the perceiver of knowledge, mechanism of perception, and object of perception, come together and, like a flawless crystal, take the color of its background."

The traditional notions of perceiver, perceived object, and mechanism of perception all depend on the illusion that we are separate from the environment, even in the act of perception. When the mind is still, this illusion evaporates and our processes of knowing are unified. We are then capable of fully experiencing the present moment.

It is striking that Patañjali uses this particular metaphor of the flawless crystal. By thinking of our mental processes as a flawless crystal that merely assumes the colors of what is nearby, he changes the frame of reference from the brain being the source of our experience to the environment being the source. Uncolored by passion, wish, or anxiety, the crystal takes on the qualities of its environment. We say: "I see," as we are performing something, casting our glance on the world. But we do not actually "see" because we do not act on the environment. Light hits an object and then enters our eyes. We receive the light and interpret the pattern. The source of our seeing *is* the light.

And yet, what happens when the environment obscures the light? We may say: "We do not see." Yet *we* are not the cause of the action. This is an illusion of ego. As an experiment, try sitting in a pitch black space with your eyes wide open and observe your mind. The distinct categories of perceiver, perceived object, and the mechanism of perception are unified when the mind is still.

LINE 42

तत्र शब्दार्थज्ञानविकल्पैः संकीर्णा सवितर्का समापत्तिः

।।१:४२।।

tatra śabdārthajñānavikalpaiḥ saṃkīrṇā savitarkā samāpattiḥ
(1:42)
tatra śabda-artha-jñāna-vikalpaiḥ saṃkīrṇā savitarkā samāpattiḥ

tatra: then
śabda: word, sound
artha: meaning
jñāna: perceptual knowledge
vikalpaiḥ: imagination
saṃkīrṇā: constricted
savitarkā: type of samadhi in which awareness of object and its designation comes into awareness
samāpattiḥ: refined attention

"A type of samādhi where the awareness is narrowed to an object's word, meaning, perceptual and imaginative categories all at once, is called savitarkā samādhi."

Our conventional words and images are all representations of reality, which activate different regions of the brain. This is a type of attention that can provide insight. However, to activate these parts of the brain *simultaneously* requires a certain type of attentional focus: *savitarkā samādhi*. This is a type of awareness in which the word, the word's meaning, our imagination of this meaning, and perceptual knowledge of an object, are united. The finger that points at the moon is not the moon. The map is not the territory.

True experience of reality does not require any linguistic categories or indicators. We do not need to post a picture on social media for an experience to be real. In fact, just the opposite: true experience reverberates in a person's character regardless of whether anyone has witnessed or represented it. This is because linguistic forms are sustained within the limits of representation and memory, both of which mediate between the individual and his or her awareness of the present moment.

LINE 43

स्मृतिपरिशुद्धौ स्वरूपशून्येवार्थमात्रनिर्भासा निर्वितर्का

।।१:४३।।

smṛtipariśuddhau svarūpaśūnyevārthamātranirbhāsā nirvitarkā
(1:43)
smṛti-pariśuddhau sva-rūpa-śūnya-iva-artha-mātra-nirbhāsa
nirvitarkā

smṛti: memory
pariśuddhau: purified
sva: one's
rūpa: form
śūnya: empty
iva: as if, like
artha: meaning, object
mātra: mere, only
nirbhāsa: shining
nirvitarkā: type of refined awareness in which contemplation of one's form is empty of memory, words, and meaning

"Nirvitarkā samādhi is a type of refined awareness devoid of memory, words and meaning, leaving only a single shining object."

We are now moving beyond the current attentional categories employed by western cognitive science. The attentional state of *nirvitarkā* moves beyond linguistic representation and memory. *Nirvitarkā* is spontaneous interaction with the world, pure and direct.

LINE 44

एतयैव सविचारा निर्विचारा च सूक्ष्मविषया व्याख्याता

।।१:४४।।

etayaiva savicārā nirvicārā ca sūkṣmaviṣayā vyākhyātā (1:44)
etayā-iva savicārā nirvicārā ca sūkṣma-viṣayā vyākhyātā

etayā: in the same way
iva: also
savicārā: type of samādhi in which word, meaning, and emotion are contemplated
nirvicārā: awareness without word, meaning, and emotion
ca: and
sūkṣma: subtle
viṣayā: objects
vyākhyātā: defined, explained

"In the same way, subtle objects are defined and explained by these types of awareness: savicārā and nirvicārā samādhi."

There are two types of attentional awareness: one with thought (*savicārā*) and the other without thought (*nirvicārā*). *Savicārā* is a type of awareness that utilizes language and its symbols. Subtle objects, such as emotional states, can be examined after the experience through analysis or be reflected upon with descriptive language. *Nirvicārā* is defined in terms of direct experience unmediated by language and symbolic thought. By directly experiencing something like anger, joy, or love, we begin to know emotions in a manner that is more presently engaged and experiential (*nirvicārā*) than through the use of language (*savicārā*).

The cultivation of these attentional skills provides the tools for validating and integrating subjective experience into one's life.[15] Even if one cannot measure subtle objects, such as emotional states, one can still come to know them by engaging these two types of attentional awareness. Therefore, the training and mastery of attentional awareness provides insight and understanding of subtle phenomena as they arise within our bodies.

---

[15] In the scientific investigation of one's own consciousness, Patañjali's method integrates one's own subjective experience as a valid means of knowledge. Phenomenology, a philosophical style of thought begun in early 20th century Europe, emphasizes subjective experience instead of the "objective" data of scientific positivism. It bases itself within the individual in order to understand and discover the world. Patañjali provides a bridge between these two conflicting schools of Western philosophy.

LINE 45

सूक्ष्मविषयत्वं चालिङ्गपर्यवसानम् ।।१:४५।।

sūkṣmaviṣayatvaṃ cāliṅgaparyavasānam (1:45)
sūkṣma-viṣayatvaṃ ca-aliṅga-paryavasānam

sūkṣma: subtle
viṣayatvaṃ: subject-ness, objectiveness
ca: and
aliṅga: formless
paryavasānam: up to

"One can deeply contemplate any object from the most subtle to the most gross, up to the formless."

Patañjali continues to describe and outline the boundaries of two types of awareness: *savicārā* and *nirvicārā*. The combined and judicious use of these attentional skills expands our capacity to move beyond objects and into more abstract realms of comprehension.

LINE 46

ता एव सबीजः समाधिः ।।१:४६।।

tā eva sabījaḥ samādhiḥ (1:46)
tā eva sabījaḥ samādhiḥ

tā: those
eva: also
sabījaḥ: with seed
samādhiḥ: refined awareness

"Those (forms of awareness) are all sabīja samādhi, still liable to fluctuation and bondage."

In the 45th line, Patañjali expands the definition of the first two types of attentional awareness. In the 46th, he provides the limits of what can be known. Both *savicāra* and *nirvicāra* states will sharpen one's ability to know the environment, but one's character will remain bound to the fluctuations of conditioned existence. These states are still influenced by mental and physical factors, such as one's imagination (mental) as well as sleep and proper cortical arousal (physical).

LINE 47

निर्विचारवैशारद्येऽध्यात्मप्रसादः ।।१:४७।।

nirvicāravaiśāradye'dhyātmaprasādaḥ (1:47)
nirvicāra-vaiśāradye-adhyātma-prasādaḥ

nirvicāra: without thought, emotion, imagination
vaiśāradye: mastery
adhyātma: toward one's self
prasādaḥ: serenity

"Mastery of the nirvicāra samādhi leads to serenity toward the self."

Meditation can lead to both serenity and insight. Mastery of *nirvicāra* leads to deep serenity, where a calm mind is the de facto state. While this can bring about profound wisdom, there is still one more stage in the development of attention. Patañjali introduces this final stage of insight in the following passages.

LINE 48

ऋतम्भरा तत्र प्रज्ञा ।।१:४८।।

ṛtambharā tatra prajñā (1:48)
ṛta-bharā tatra prajñā

ṛta: the natural order of the world, reality
bharā: carrying, supporting
tatra: then
prajñā: wisdom, free from error

"Then, one's wisdom is synchronized with the natural order of the world."

When one is calibrated with the natural world, observing carefully and interacting with skillful means, one has achieved the apex of adaptive function. These are the skills needed to navigate the world. Wisdom arrives when the boundaries between one's individual self and the outer environment are both fluid and precise. This happens through close observation of the gateways of perception and attention that mediate between the body and the environment.[16]

---

[16] Jurgen Aschoff & H. Pohl, "Phase relations between a circadian rhythm and its zeitgeber within the range of entrainment." *Naturwissenschafen* 65 (1978): 80-84.

LINE 49

श्रुतानुमानप्रज्ञाभ्यामन्यविषया विशेषार्थत्वात् ।।१:४९।।

śrutānumānaprajñābhyāmanyaviṣayā viśeṣārthatvāt (1:49)
śruta-anumāna-prajñābhyām-anya-viṣayā viśeṣa-arthatvāt

śruta: hearing, auditory memory
anumāna: inference
prajñābhyām: practice of wisdom
anya: other, different
viṣayā: subject
viśeṣa: special, beyond the ordinary
arthatvāt: due to its significance

"This practice of wisdom is spontaneous, direct, and extraordinary, different from knowledge via hearing, memory and inference."

Here Patañjali describes the type of wisdom that emerges with mastery of *nirvicāra* and *savicāra* attentional states. This is not the type of intelligence that relies on reasoning and sharp memory. Rather, this state requires full presence in an ongoing interaction with the world free from the biases of memory and reason. As these types of attention become automatic over time, one's character becomes wise, playful, and spontaneous.

LINE 50

तज्जः संस्कारोऽन्यसंस्कारप्रतिबन्धी ॥१:५०॥

tajjaḥ saṃskāro'anyasaṃskārapratibandhī (1:50)
tajjaḥ saṃskāraḥ-anya-saṃskāraḥ-pratibandhī

tajjaḥ: born from that, based on
saṃskāraḥ: subtle impression based on memory
anya: other
pratibandhī: remove, dominate

"As this newly developed mental quality strengthens, it will dominate the reflexive tendencies of misapprehension."

As a person learns a new behavior that serves him or her more effectively, the previous approach will naturally go away. As taste for high-quality attention becomes more refined, a person will find these types of attention more enjoyable and replace previous impressions based on memory. This creates a positive feedback loop that reinforces the new behavior.

LINE 51

तस्यापि निरोधे सर्वनिरोधान्निर्बीजः समाधिः ।।१:५१।।

tasyāpi nirodhe sarvanirodhānnirbījaḥ samādhiḥ (1:51)
tasyāpi nirodhe sarva-nirodhāt-nirbījaḥ samādhiḥ

tasya: these
āpi: and, also
nirodhe: inhibited
sarva: all
nirodhāt: inhibition
nirbījaḥ: without seeds, seedless
samādhiḥ: refined attention

"Nirbīja samādhi is when even the inhibition of the mind is inhibited."

This final state of *samādhi* is a transcendent state of being in which the mind knows itself. *Nirbīja samādhi* is a type of awareness free from the cycle of cause and effect. So long as a seed exists, it is capable of bearing more karmic fruit, which manifests as more bondage. *Nirbīja* translates as "seedless." Thus, our actions are free from their repercussions. "All matter is merely energy condensed to a slow vibration, that we are all one consciousness experiencing itself subjectively, there is no such thing as death, life is only a dream, and we are the imagination of ourselves."[17]

[17] "Quotable Quote," Quote by Bill Hicks, Goodreads, accessed September 2, 2020. https://www.goodreads.com/quotes/8870-today-a-young-man-on-acid-realized-that-all-matter.

LINE 52

इतिप्रधामः पदः

iti pradhāmaḥ padaḥ (1:52)

"Here ends the Foundations of Samādhi."

Now that we have completed the *Foundations of Samādhi*, we understand the theoretical framework for the three types of attentional awareness. The next three books examine these types of attention in practice. The final goal of Patañjali's yogic method is a direct experience of true freedom.

Appendix

Principles of Neuroplasticity based on Patañjali's *Yoga Sūtra*:

1. Neuroplasticity depends upon a specific neural electrical pattern. This pattern is marked by a specific autonomic signature to changes as a behavior becomes fully internalized.

2. Neuroplasticity requires practice and effort.

3. Meditative absorption emerges with steady effort.

4. Necessary pre-requisites for neuroplastic change include: repetition, synchronized activation of voice and touch, reflection, and active cognitive discrimination.

5. The steps of neuroplastic transformation can be understood within the framework of the nine stages of sādhana: intention, skillful means, conscious application of breathing, awareness and control of posture, *dhāraṇa, dhyāna, samādhi,* and *saṃyama.*

6. Deep mindfulness is attained when one distinguishes between the different types of attention and masters the appropriate application of each.

Bibliography

Apte, Vanam Shivaram. *The Practical Sanskrit-English Dictionary.* Kyoto: Rinsen Press, 1957.

Aschoff, Jurgen and H. Pohl. "Phase relations between a circadian rhythm and its zeitgeber within the range of entrainment." *Naturwissenschafen* 65 (1978).

Da Vinci, Leonardo. *Leonardo Da Vinci on Painting: A Lost Book.* California: University of California Press, 1965.

Davidson, Richard J., Lawrence L. Greischar, Nancy B. Rawlings, Matthieu Ricard, and Antoine Lutz. "Long-Term Meditators Self-Induce High-Amplitude Gamma Synchrony during Mental Practice." *Proceedings of the National Academy of Sciences of the United States of America* 101, no. 46 (2004).

Freud, Sigmund. *Interpretation of Dreams,* trans. Dr. A. A. Brill. New York: Modern Library Edition, 1994.

Goodreads. "Quotable Quote." Quote by Bill Hicks. Accessed September 2, 2020. https://www.goodreads.com/

quotes/8870-today-a-young-man-on-acid-realized-that-all-matter

Goodreads. "Quotable Quote." Quote by Mizuta Masahide. Accessed September 2, 2020. https://www.goodreads.com/quotes/631601-since-my-house-burned-down-i-now-have-a-better

Kuriyama, Shigehisa. *The Expressiveness of the Body.* New York: Zone Books, 1999.

Merriam-Webster Dictionary. "Babinski reflex," accessed September 2, 2020, https://www.merriam-webster.com/dictionary/Babinski%20reflex.

Merzenich, M., E. Temple, G. K. Deutsch, R. A. Poldrack, S. L. Miller, P. Tallal, J. D. Gabrieli. "Neural deficits in children with dyslexia ameliorated by behavioral remediation: Evidence from functional MRI." *Proceedings of the National Academy of Sciences* 100, no. 5 (2003).

Quine, W.O. *Word and Object*. Cambridge: MIT Press, 1960.

Russell, Bertand. *Wisdom of the West*. Garden City, NY: Doubleday, 1959.

Sherrington, Sir Charles. “Inhibition as a Coordinative Factor.” Nobel Lecture, Stockholm, December 10, 1932.

ABOUT THE AUTHORS

Shaun Nanavati is a neuroscience researcher, professor, and clinician with an interest in Eastern philosophy. He is the Founder and Chief Science Officer at Mindwell Labs, whose mission is to provide highly customized mindful awareness services. He is on the faculty at the Nalanda Institute and previously taught Cognitive Psychology at CUNY.

Shaun has graduate degrees in both Eastern and Western inner sciences. These include an M.A. in Comparative World Religion from Columbia University and a Research and Design Master's from the New School for Social Research. He is also trained in clinical neuropsychology. He has published papers and given presentations on visual perception, the neuroscience of yoga, and mindfulness meditation.

Sam Aldridge is a seeker of all things beneath and beyond the sky. A recent graduate from Columbia University, he studied postcolonial theory in the context of South Asia with a focus on the politics of history and translation. He has studied and practiced yoga since he was 16 when he lived in India, and he enjoys playing the sitar at his home in Oneonta, N.Y.

Printed in Great Britain
by Amazon

58911027R00056